The Wind in My Ears

Milly Brown

summersdale

THE WIND IN MY EARS

Summersdale Publishers Ltd
46 West Street
Chichester
West Sussex
PO19 1RP
UK

www.summersdale.com

Printed and bound in China

ISBN: 978-1-84953- 480-2

Substantial discounts on bulk quantities of Summersdale books are available to corporations, professional associations and other organisations. For details contact Nicky Douglas by telephone: +44 (0) 1243 756902, fax: +44 (0) 1243 786300 or email: nicky@summersdale.com.

To..

From..

Freedom never tasted
so good

Doggles on. Check.
Safety harness in place. Check.
Driver, I'm all set, step on it.

Engage flaps

CCCHHHAAARRRGGGEEE!

Notice how I angle my ears back for maximum speed

I'm giving a whole new meaning to the words 'doggy bag'

Oh, the joys of spring

I love a good trip to the salon followed
by nature's blow-dry

Look, that spot right there is where
we first met

I'm loving this! I can't see but I'm loving it!

Before we go, are you sure health and safety approved this?

Who's da man? I's da man

Sunbathing for the dog on the go

OK – the indicator's on and you can now turn right

Shall we play Chariots of Fire?

This puppy's gonna drive...

Does anyone else feel carsick?

You seen chickens?! Stop the car!

I'm ready; crank up the engine

I feel the need for speed

If only I could reach the pedals...

FMLGHFMLGHH – someone get these ears out my mouth!

Watch what happens when I stick my tongue out at the kid in the car behind...

All the freewheeling dogs put your
paws up

Less parking, more speed!

I'm flying, Jack, I'm really flying!

Breezy does it

The whistle of the wind makes
a fine tune

Born to be wild!

PHOTO ACKNOWLEDGEMENTS

Summersdale Publishers Ltd would like to thank everyone (dogs included!) who gave us permission to use their photo in *The Wind in My Ears*. In order of appearance in the book, our appreciations go to:

Tom Wang, Shutterstock

Frannie Metz for their photo of Zilla

Mariia Masich, Shutterstock

Stephen Mcsweeny, Shutterstock

German Pardo for their photo of Indy

James L. Davidson, Shutterstock

Lobke Peers, Shutterstock

crazychris84, Shutterstock

Luke J. Rosynek for their photo of Sofie and Professor Kato Barkington

David MacFarlane, Shutterstock

Marcel Jancovic, Shutterstock

Dwight Smith, Shutterstock

Charro Badger, In the Sun Studio, for their photo of Lincoln

Yelena Shister for their photo of Cuba

Matthew John 85, Shutterstock

Mikeledray, Shutterstock

Annette Shaff, Shutterstock

GJS, Shutterstock

SueC, Shutterstock

Krista Meyer for their photo of Dusty

Dave Brigham

Sean MacLeay, Shutterstock

Kim Whalen for their photo of Sasha

Candace Schwadron, Shutterstock

Bruce Amos, Shutterstock

AnetaPics, Shutterstock

Bill Binns for their photo of Dave

Karen A. Smith for their photo of Sunny

Geoff Hardy, Shutterstock

Is your dog a star in the making? Does he/she ooze canine charm? Send us a picture of them to auntie@summersdale.com in their most handsome, funny or cute pose for a chance to appear in one of our books. You will also be entered into a prize draw with some tail-waggingly good Summersdale treats up for grabs.

See www.summersdale.com/blog/competition for terms and conditions.

Twitter: @Summersdale
Facebook: Summersdale Publishers

www.summersdale.com